From Idea to Publication

How to Self-Publish Your Book With No Upfront Cost

Rosetta Jamieson-Thomas

Rosetta Jamieson-Thomas

Copyright © 2015 Rosetta Jamieson Thomas.

All rights reserved.

No part of this book may be used or reproduced by any means: graphic, electronic or mechanical, including photocopying, recording, taping, or by any information storage retrieval system without the written permission of the publisher, except in the case of brief quotations embodied in critical articles and reviews.

Island Novel Publishing is a division of Divine Word Communications, LLC, a publisher and promoter of Christian literature. Our products can be purchased in bulk at a discounted price. Please contact us for details at (973) 943-1743; write to us at island_novel@yahoo.com or visit our website at www.empoweredpages.com

Printed in the United States of America

ISBN: 0991643348

ISBN-13: 978-0-9916433-4-9

DEDICATION

For my Grandchildren

CONTENTS

Acknowledgments

Introduction   5

1. Independent Publishing vs. Bundled Self-Publishing Services   9
    i. Ownership & Control
    ii. The Process & The Proceeds
    iii. Pricing
    iv. Revenue From Book Sales

2. Protect Your Rights   16
    i. Rights & Publishing Agreements
    ii. Copyright
    iii. Giving & Receiving Permission

3. Is Your Writing A Hobby or A Business?   21
    i. Register Your Business
    ii. Create A Business Plan

4. Self-Publishing: Are You Up To The Task?   28
    i. Task Analysis: Stages of Publication
    ii. Realistic Self-Assessment

5. Create Your DIY Publishing Team   35
    I.
        i. Choose A Publishing Platform
        ii. Print Services
        iii. Print, eBook, and Distribution Services

6. ISBN & Barcode   43

    i. Buy and Use Your Own

    ii. Register Your Title

7. Turn Your Manuscript into A Book   49

    i. Create Print Ready Files

    ii. Layout and Format Your Book

    iii. Create Your Book Cover

    iv. Putting It All Together

8. Polish Before You Publish

    i. How to Self-edit Your Non-Fiction Manuscript   55

    ii. Self-edit Your Novel

    iii. Self-edit Your Book Cover

9. Ready to Publish   63

10. Publish & Publicize Your Book

Last Words

Resources

About the Author

Books by Rosetta Jamieson-Thomas

Books By Shauna Jamieson Carty

ACKNOWLEDGMENTS

I want to express my sincere thanks and appreciation

To author and journalist, Shauna Jamieson Carty, who is also my daughter and writing partner, my most ardent reader, first critic and editor

To author Renee Smith who encouraged me to write this book

To my husband, Samuel, for his support, patience and understanding

To members of my writing group, SBC-Christian Writers Ministry, for their prayers, critique, support, and encouragement

To Minister Patricia G. Williams, author and the co-founder of Crossroads of Life Christian Bookstore, Hillside, New Jersey, USA, who is a strong supporter of independently published authors. Thank you, Sister Williams, for opening up your heart and your bookstore to us and our products. God bless you.

To friends, family members, and everyone who has contributed in any way to our success as independent author-publishers

To the Author and Finisher of our faith: Jesus Christ (Hebrews 12:2).

God bless you!

Rosetta Jamieson-Thomas

INTRODUCTION

Are you a writer looking to publish your first book? Are you an independent author who has paid or is paying a self-publishing service company thousands of dollars to publish your book? Do you still have boxes of unsold books left over from your last volume-discount purchase from your self-publishing service company? Do you want full control of your book from idea to publication? If you answer yes to any of these questions, then this book is written just for you!

Today, publishing options are numerous, and we are all aware of the paradigm shift in the publishing landscape. It is a dramatic shift from the totally traditional approach to "self-publishing" made possible by the ever increasing advance of technology. A spin-off from this is the proliferation of a new breed of publishers - Self-publishing Service Companies – that mimic the services of the established traditional publishers but, are really mostly vanity presses in disguise.

Aspiring authors who could not get a traditional publisher to look at their manuscript are now the ones who are being courted by self-publishing service companies. It is these authors' creative works that are fueling the self-publishing explosion. However, it is the self-publishing service companies that are cashing in on this explosion, and they are doing so by selling expensive publishing packages to aspiring authors.

Technology has given you, the aspiring author, the opportunity to ditch high-priced self-publishing packages, and independently publish your books in print, e-book or audio book format. There are many companies with self-publishing platforms that make available free tools to facilitate independent publishing if you are committed and up to the challenge. Others offer a combination of free tools and as-needed paid professional services that allow you flexibility, real choice, and control of the process as well as the proceeds from your writing. This guide will show you, step by step, how to start your writing business, choose and pay for only the services you need, and take control of every aspect of your book from idea to publication.

When I wrote my first novel I knew nothing about the self-publishing process and very little about traditional publishing. My quest for a publisher began with the purchase of a copy of the popular Writers Market Guide, an excellent annual resource book for writers of all genres. Here I found a listing of markets, publishers' guidelines, useful contact information, and instructions on how to query publishers and agents, write book proposals, prepare and submit a manuscript. I subscribed to Writers Digest Book Club and bought dozens of books on writing and publishing. I also took graduate courses leading to an M.A. in Creative Writing to polish my writing skills. I spent many hours reading guidelines and listings into which my historical romance novel, *Centre of the Labyrinth*, set in the Caribbean, would fit. There were several possibilities but I soon discovered that I must have a literary agent. Without this "mediator" between the author and the publisher there was not much chance of getting my manuscript seen by a traditional publisher.

My daughter, Shauna Jamieson Carty, also a writer, researched and queried several agents. Finally, she found an agent who agreed to represent us. You can just imagine how excited we were! She met with this agent and delivered the manuscript in person. Then we waited. Several months went by without any feed-back from the agent. Then, eventually when we got the feedback, we were not satisfied with the agent's approach. We took back the manuscript and my daughter continued her search for a publisher.

It was at this point in her research that she stumbled upon the idea of self-publishing and found a self-publishing service company that offered to publish my novel for a fee. Naturally, we were very skeptical initially. On the one hand, we were aware of the practices of "vanity publishers" and we didn't want to be stuck with paying for, stacking, storing, and marketing large quantities of books. On the other hand, self-published books were not well-received in a publishing landscape dominated by traditional publishers and traditionally published authors. Additionally, bookstores did not stock self-published books. So it seemed as if the odds were stacked against the self-publishing author right from the start. However, after several conversations and email messages with a representative of a self-publishing service company, we went for it! It was a great experience and the finished product was well worth the effort.

The self-publishing service company we used delivered what it offered in the package of services we bought. The book was professionally finished and you could not distinguish it from one that was traditionally published. However, we had one complaint. The retail price was too high. That was the first negative factor in this publishing experience. When we tried to negotiate a lower price my daughter and I realized that we were not going to have any control of my published book. To begin with, it was highly overpriced at $27.95 each, and the publisher denied our request to lower the price.

We had to settle for the author's discount that the publisher offered, and we in turn passed on most of that discount to our readers. Author's discount was available at 35% for fewer than 200 copies, and author's volume-discount of 50% to 55% for 500 or more copies. I purchased my books from the publisher at the volume-discounted price and sold them at $20.00 each. Readers' response was excellent and, despite the cost of buying my own books from the publisher at a highly inflated price, over-all it was a very successful venture into self-publishing.

Since then Self-Publishing has grown exceedingly and self-published products, in different formats are altering the publishing landscape, changing attitudes, and finding some acceptance in a world once dominated by traditional publishing. Keeping pace with this is the ever-increasing number of writers who have stopped using packages of services bundled by "self-publishers" and are operating as independent authors in control of their books.

Following up on our first venture into self-publishing my daughter and I have published several books. We did not give up the use of publishing packages immediately. In fact, together we published a total of seven books using pre-packaged services. Despite the absence of the control we wanted over our books, and the low returns on our investments, there were many valuable lessons we learnt and skills we acquired through these publishing experiences. Over time, we garnered a wealth of experience and knowledge in "self-publishing" and have moved on to becoming fully independent authors and publishers. We now write, publish, and market our books independently. By sharing our experience with you, we hope you too will be challenged to take control of your book from idea to publication.

For Thought & Discussion

1. If you are a new, or unpublished writer, why do you want to self-publish?

2. What is your goal or vision for your book?

3. How much control do you want? How much can you successfully handle?

CHAPTER ONE

Independent Publishing Versus Bundled Self-Publishing Services

Definitions

In the purest sense of the word, a self-publisher is an author who writes and publishes his/her own creative work without the assistance of an established third party publisher. However, in today's publishing world, the meaning of self-published author/self-publisher is not as clear-cut as this. In fact, self-publishing/self-publisher as used in the self-publishing industry is a misnomer, and as always, the intended meaning must be gleaned from the context.

Independent publishing occurs when the author or creator of the work is also the publisher. The independent author/publisher is one who has complete control over every aspect of the creative work, from idea to publication and marketing. Instead of buying pre-packaged services he/she exercises the option of creating her own publishing team and purchasing only the professional and technical support services he/she needs.

Bundled self-publishing services are packages of services marketed by companies in the publishing industry that call themselves "self-publishers" many of which are veiled vanity presses.

Self-Publishing Service Companies/Self-Publishers

It is true that not all self-publishing service companies are "dressed-up" vanity publishers. Some offer really good packages that include a limited amount of author-control, and many self-publishing authors who use these services are doing well. On the other hand, many self-published authors are paying out big cash up-front for the services of self-publishing companies and are getting very little return on their investment. Frankly, if your goal is to sell your books and get a good return on your investment then pre-packaged services are not what you need. Self-publishing service companies' priority is to sell you as many services as they can entice you to buy, not to promote the sale of your books.

Worst case scenario: you spend $1000.00 on a basic publishing package, and at the end of the publishing process, you get 3 copies of your published book "for free" and zero ownership and control of the digital files. You can't print any more books from these files which you paid the self-publishing service company to prepare, because the files are not available to you. Unless you have more money to invest in purchasing additional copies of your books at the price set by the self-publishing service company you will never see another copy of your print book. You have just sank a thousand dollars into three books!

If you, the aspiring writer, want to use a self-publishing service company because it's a quick and easy way to publish your book, do the research before you commit. But know that even the few companies that claim to offer "full author control" and "100% royalty" do so in the context of their bundled services that come with hefty price tags. (For an excellent and enlightening side-by-side comparison of several self-publishing service companies, read Mark Levine, *The Fine Print of Self-Publishing*)

Ownership and Control

For those of you who have paid an established self-publishing service company to publish your books, how much control did you have over the publication process? And how much control do you have over the proceeds? You started out with the purchase of a package of services compiled by the self-publishing company and what is included in that package varies depending on how much you pay for the package.

Additionally, some of the services included in the package are things you could have done yourself.

When you, the independent author, are also the independent publisher you have complete control of both the process (writing, production and marketing) and full control of the proceeds. When you buy a package of services from a self-publishing service company you hand over your finished manuscript for the company to convert into a book, as per the services offered by the package you bought. Your package offers "custom cover design" but you write the back cover copy yourself and if you want assistance with this, it may cost you an additional $199.00 for a "cover copy polish." That is, the self-publishing service company will tweak your original a little – maybe, rearrange a sentence or two, for that price. You get one round of proof and with this you can make very limited changes. If you need to change anything beyond the limit of what is allowed, that will be at an additional cost to you.

Pre-Packaged Services

Most, if not all of us as independent authors started our publishing journey with bundled self-publishing packages. It is expensive but it is the quick and easy way to get published. Self-publishing is a highly competitive marketplace, and some "self-publishers" do offer the author a little more than other self-publishers do, but the underlying principles are the same. Packages range in prices from the very basic/minimal service package for a few hundred dollars to gold/platinum/diamond packages costing thousands of dollars. It is the self-publishing service companies that define the terms of service and what the packages offer. When you add to this the terms and conditions of the Publishing Agreement which the self-publisher drafts and you, the author, sign, it's obvious the self-publishers are in complete control of your creative work, and stand to earn more from your efforts than you do.

Generally, what you pay for is what you get (or less). If you can afford it and want to invest in the most expensive packages, then you will definitely get more services than the person who is publishing on a low budget. However, whether you buy a $299.00 or $10,000.00 package, you do not have control of your digital files and you cannot make changes, add services, or print more books without additional cost.

Each package comes with a limited number of "free" books included. Currently, iUniverse, includes 3 "free soft cover books" with its $999.00 package and 20 with its $4,399.00. So, how much does it cost you to produce one 6x9 trade paperback book using iUniverse basic package? Do the math! Beyond that, the self-publisher gives you a discount when you buy copies of your own book for sales, reviews, book launch, etc.

With most of these self-publishing service companies you, the author, do not own your production files, the cover design or interior files used to print your book even though you've paid the publishing company to create these. iUniverse, for instance, makes this clear by inserting the iUniverse watermark on every page of the proof it prepares for you. If you decide to leave iUniverse, and you want these files, you must pay for them.... again!

As an independent publisher you own all your books and you control your digital files. You can choose to print as many or as few of your books as you want and as often as you want (at the cost of printing only); and you have the option to do with them exactly what pleases you: sell them at a price you set, or give them as gifts. You do not have this flexibility when you use bundled self-publishing service.

No matter how much you pay for your "publishing package", in the end, all you have to show for your initial cash layout and the hundreds of hours you may have spent writing and preparing your manuscript, is the number of so-called "free" books you bought in your package. This may vary from 1 to 20 "free" books, depending on the package of services you bought.

At the time of writing this, iUniverse offered 3 "free" soft cover books with the Select package at a cost of $999.00 and 20 'free" books with the $4,399.00 package. I have worked with both the Select and the Premier packages at a time when they cost much less than they do today. But the process is the same. The goal of Self-Publishing Service Companies is to sell services.

When it comes to using packaged self-publishing services where you really get hit hard is in the checkbook, especially if you start with a basic package and you need to purchase the "add-on" services. For example, copyright registration, offered as an add-on to a basic package will cost you $170.00 at iUniverse. You can register your copyright yourself at a cost of $35.00 for online electronic filing and $85.00 for a mailed-in paper application, plus two copies of your book.

Self-publishing service companies do not read your manuscript (unless you purchase a package that includes editorial service), but for an additional fee of about $599.00 you can add on an editorial evaluation. For this price iUniverse, for example, will read your manuscript, tell you what errors are in your manuscript, and charge you an additional fee for editing. How much this will cost you varies with the level of editing your manuscript needs.

I use iUniverse packages as my point of reference because my daughter and I have published seven titles with iUniverse (4 full length novels, 2 devotional books and 1 non-fiction book). I know several authors who have used iUniverse services and you yourself may have published with iUniverse. Despite the cost of the services, the absence of author control, and the low royalty, we re-used iUniverse's book production services because we had no problem getting professionally finished products in a timely manner.

Bundled self-publishing service, on the front-end, is quick and easy. That is why so many new authors and some experienced authors select this option. But in the long run, the disadvantages far out-weigh the advantages of speed and ease. As an independent author you need to understand the publishing process to be able to make informed choices. You need to know what services it is advantageous for you to purchase, and which you can and should do for yourself. There is no excuse for paying massive up-front cost for what you can do for your self (with the aid of free publishing tools). There is also no excuse for not purchasing the services you really need to give your book that professionally polished finish it needs.

Pricing

When you publish using packaged self-publishing service you have little or no control over the market price of your books. The company sets the retail price of your books and this is generally nonnegotiable. Very often your self-published book is priced out of the market, and in order to sell the ones you purchase from the self-publishing service company, you may have to mark-down these to 50% below the price set by the publisher. - at a loss to you. Some self-publishing service companies that give you a say in the pricing of your book will tell you that the higher you set your price is the more you will make on your investment. What they fail to tell you is that you may be pricing your book out of the market for your genre. As an independent publisher you set your own retail price; one that will allow your print book to remain viable in a highly competitive market dominated by e-readers and digital content, and still get a good return on your investment. In Chapter 5 we will discuss book pricing and royalty in the context of the self-publishing services offered by CreateSpace and IngramSpark.

Royalty or Revenue from Book Sales

You, the author, receives from the self-publishing company, in the form of royalty, a percentage of the revenue from the company's sale of your books, as specified in the Publishing Agreement. But you get no royalty on the books you purchase from the self-publishing company. Instead the company sells you, the author, your books at a discounted rate which is predicated on whether or not the self-publishing company is running a 'volume discount" promotion. Basic author discount is usually 30% to 40% and up to 60% for volume discounted purchases of 2000 or more books. In other words, if you buy a lot of your books at one time the sale price to you is discounted at up to 60% off the market price for bulk orders. But in computing your royalty, the publisher does not include the number of books you buy. These are described as "royalty exclusive". This is standard practice for the self-publishing industry.

So, if you're the biggest buyer of your books, how much revenue can you really generate from publishing through self-publishing service companies? Do you really want to warehouse hundreds of your books that you may never sell? It's your loss, not theirs. Author purchases are non-refundable.

Rights and Publishing Agreement

The independent author/publisher owns all rights to the creative work. When you engage a self-publishing company to produce and market your work you must relinquish some rights to that publisher.

Non-exclusive and Exclusive Rights

What you, the author, need to give to the publisher is the **non-exclusive** right to publish your work. Never the **Exclusive Right**. As the author you retain the Exclusive Right.

Generally, the self-publishing company will ask for nothing more than the non-exclusive rights but it is your responsibility to find out exactly what is contained in that. Most will want the right or license to publish your book in print format and/or e-book format while others may ask for more. You should get all the details laid out in a formal written and signed agreement between you and the publisher.

Publishing Agreement

Self-publishing Service companies do not give you a Publishing Agreement upfront and you do not get to preview this before you buy the package. The company will have the publishing agreement for the package of services you buy on its website. After you purchase the package be sure to download and print this out. Read it carefully, and if you are not in agreement with the terms you can cancel the purchase of your bundle of services *before* your book publication process begins. When you accept and sign a Publishing Agreement be sure to keep a hard copy for your file.

The disadvantages of using bundled self–publishing services far outweigh the benefits to you, the author. You will find it is easy to use these bundled services because you do not have to do much more than upload your manuscript to a self-service publisher, but this is not cost effective. You pay more for less. However, whether you choose to purchase a package of services from a self-publishing company or not will depend on your vision and goal for your book as well as your level of commitment to doing most of the work yourself.

For Thought & Discussion

1. *If you have published using packaged services or if you are an independent DIY author-publisher describe your experience.*

_____
_____
_____

2. *What would you do differently?*

CHAPTER TWO

Protect Your Rights

What is Copyright?

Copyright is a form of legal protection given to you, the author/creator of your book or of any other creative work independently produced by you and exists in a fixed, tangible form, for example your book, poetry, movies, videos, photographs, etc.

Copyright is automatic. That is, as soon as you start writing your book you own the copyright to what you have written, published or unpublished. It's your intellectual property.

Copyright does not protect your book title or ideas.

Copyright gives you, the owner, the exclusive rights to produce copies of your work for distribution and sale to the public; to create derivative works based on your original creation; to publicly display or perform the creative work; to transfer ownership or permit use by others.

Copyright Notice

Always put a copyright notice in your book, immediately following the title page. A copyright notice alerts others that your work is legally protected under your country's copyright laws. A copyright notice consists of three segments:
1. Copyright symbol © that is a c in a circle
2. The date the work was first published
3. The name of the copyright owner

You should also add : *All Rights Reserved.*

Most publications also carries this statement, *"No part of this book may be used or reproduced by any means: graphic, electronic or mechanical, including photocopying, recording, taping, or by any information storage retrieval system without the written permission of the publisher, except in the case of brief quotations embodied in critical articles and reviews."*

Copyright Registration

Copyright registration is optional but strongly recommended. It is a way of publicly recording your right of ownership. It also provides you with documented proof of ownership should there be any infringement of such rights resulting in legal action.

How to Register Your Copyright

To register your copyright in USA you need to file an application with the US Copyright Office and submit two copies of your published work. You may apply online at http://www.copyright.gov or complete and mail the paper Registration Form TX . Registration fee is currently $35.00 for online registration and $85.00 for paper registration.

To file online: log on to copyright.gov website and select eCO Registration system. Here you will find a tutorial that walks you through the steps for filing a basic registration. If you are a first time user, complete the tutorial.

When you are ready to start your application click on **Register a Copyright**. You will be asked to log in (User name & password) or register (first time user) and complete personal information to access the electronic copyright office registration system.

To file Form TX by mail and submit mandatory deposit of two copies of your work, download the form. Complete it on your computer, print and mail, with the appropriate payment to

>Library of Congress
>US Copyright Office
>101 Independence Avenue, SE
>Washington DC 20559

Readers outside the USA should check the copyright regulations or your country of residence.

Giving & Receiving Permission

You may use limited portion of the work of others, and they yours, without written permission, but strictly for non-commercial use. This is considered *fair use*. For anything beyond that you must obtain permission from the copyright owner in writing (and you must give permission in writing.) In some instances, you may even need signed, notarized permission to use the material.

Some works (usually over 75 years old) have become part of what is known as *public domain* and can be used without permission if they are free of copyright restrictions. It is always best to check, even when a work is classified as public domain, as in some cases the copyright might have been renewed.

A Word About Creative Commons Licenses & Copyright Permission

As the creator of creative content you have exclusive right, under copyright law, to your creative works and the right to use it in any legal way you choose. What Creative Commons, a nonprofit organization founded in 2001, does is to encourage the sharing of intellectual property by simplifying the way permission is granted and received for use of the works of others, without copyright infringement.

A statement on Creative Commons website, http://creativecommons.org, reads, "Our tools give everyone from individual creators to large companies and institutions a simple, standardized way to grant copyright permission to their creative work" and Creative Commons "provide a pool of content that can be copied, distributed, edited, remixed, and built upon – all within the boundaries of copyright law." A copyright holder can register his work with Creative Commons, restricts the purposes for which his work is used, and maintain copyright. He can also contribute his work for public domain use, with no rights reserved.

If you are interested in knowing more about Creative Commons licenses, visit the Creative Commons website.

Your Book Copyright Page

The copyright page of your book is the page immediately behind the title page. It is a very important page and you should be sure to include this page in your book. Here is what to put on the copyright page.

The book title and three-part copyright statement, and usually a specific statement pertaining to the use of any part of this publication

Example: *Twilight Tryst*
A novel
Copyright © 2015 by Jill Romance
All rights reserved. No part of this book may be used or reproduced by any means: graphic, electronic, or mechanical, including photocopying, recording, taping, or by any information storage device without the written permission of the publisher except in the case of brief quotations embodied in critical articles and reviews.

Add the publisher's information

Published by The Twilight Press, 25 Romance Way, Novel City, Name of State and Country, contact information (phone number, website or email address, and edition (if applicable)

A disclaimer:. For a work of fiction this may read
This is a work of fiction . All characters, names, incidents, organization, and dialogue in this novel is a product of the authors imagination and/or used fictitiously

Give credit for any material you had permission to use, for example, if you quote from the Bible, don't assume it is Public Domain. Different publishing houses own the copyright to the various translations. State the translation and copyright date, and used by permission of . . . .Check the copyright page of the Bible from which you quoted. Most of the new translations tell you how to ascribe the credit. Similarly, if you get permission for use of material, including graphics, from other sources you must credit these on your copyright page.

The all-important ISBN (13 digits) and the Library of Congress Control Number also go on this page.

If you publish your book in print and in digital format you need a separate ISBN for each format. You may put both ISBN on this page and indicate which is for the print book and which is for the e-book.

CHAPTER THREE

Is Writing Your Hobby or Your Business?

You have a great idea for a book so you have been writing for months, maybe years. Finally, you have written the last sentence, added the final period, and those magical last words: The End! You gave a sigh of relief, stretched and flexed your tired fingers that have been hacking at the computer keyboard all these hundreds of hours. You are mentally exhausted but excited. There is no denying the rush! Finished and ready to publish ...

Hold on! Not so fast!

You do not have a book yet. You have a manuscript, or to be more specific, you have the first draft of your manuscript. Congratulations! You are at the end of the beginning!

I believe that, even before you wrote the first word of your manuscript, you knew what you wanted to write (novel, short story, poetry, drama, biography, etc.). You also had a pretty good idea of the readers you want to reach. For most of us, the major question is not what to write or for whom to write. Usually, it's a question of how do I publish what I write.

So often you hear others say, "I know I have at least one book in me." And I imagine they do, given a life-time of experiences. So the problem is not finding what to write about. With a little imagination, the possibilities are endless – one can draw from a wealth of personal experiences, family history, vacations, the environment, the people you meet every day, family photos, unexpected encounters. You name it! The sources of inspirations are numerous.

Your Hobby or Your Business?

You must decide right from the start whether your writing is your hobby or your business. If your writing is a hobby you are writing because you like to write, you enjoy writing, and the satisfaction you get from this is all you need. You write when you feel like writing. You may choose to keep your writing private, or you may choose to publish and share it with friends and family members.

When your writing is a hobby and not a business the decisions you make about publishing (or not publishing) your work are not that crucial. You may choose to make your own copies to distribute among family and friends, or use a book printing or packaged self-publishing service. You do not need to buy an ISBN. You can accept a free ISBN if the self-publisher offers one or you can publish without an ISBN. You are not concerned about book sales or revenue from your writing. Your published book is your reward.

Your Writing As Your Business

Writing as a business is a demanding, time-consuming and expensive business. And when you decide to write and publish independently your investment of time and money can be tremendous. Writing as your business is also a rewarding and satisfying adventure and, for all aspiring writers, a successful writing business is a dream come true.

First Things First

Before you jump in and invest large amount of time and money into self – publishing get the lay of the land. Know what's out there in the publishing world, and understand what you are getting into. Be informed. Knowledge is power.

So, before you invest:

>   Survey

>   Question

>   Research

>   Find Your Niche

>   Plan

There are volumes of free information and free writing tools and resources available to help you grow your writing business. Find them, use them, and don't forget to credit your sources.

Do not limit yourself to online information only. Do some bookstore browsing. Know your audience and what interest them and know your competition as well. There are volumes of books on the market in your genre and yours will be competing with theirs for the readers' dollars. A great way to survey what's out there in your genre and assess your competition is by browsing what's on the shelves in the physical bookstores as well as online major booksellers like Amazon and Barnes and Noble. Also check out sites like Goodreads to see what others are reading and commenting on.

While browsing in bookstores and the book sections in major stores like Walmart and Target know exactly what you're looking for. Don't just look for any fiction or non-fiction books. Zero in on categories in your genre, for example, if you are writing a novel know exactly what you are writing. Is it romance, mystery, adventure, etc.? Check out the covers. What do they look like? Flip through the book. Read the back cover, author bio, readers' reviews or any endorsement. If browsing on Amazon use the look inside the book feature. Read a selection. How is the book similar or different from yours? Why should readers buy your book? What are you offering your readers that is not already available to them? Do an honest assessment. Is what you're seeing better than what you are writing? Not as good as yours or just about the same?

I can hear you thinking as you read this, "Who has time for all that? I just want to finish writing my book and get it published." That is fine if your writing is your hobby. But if it is your business then knowing your audience and your competition is an essential part of your journey into successful independent publishing.

My Notes

_____
_____
_____
_____
_____
_____
_____
_____
_____
_____
_____
_____
_____
_____
_____
_____
_____
_____
_____
_____

CREATE A BUSINESS PLAN

Create a business plan? I know you may well be thinking that this is premature. Why create a business plan when all you have so far is the first draft of a manuscript and/or a couple of books you paid thousands of dollars to publish? Books you are still trying to sell to recover your investment cost and hopefully, to make a profit. Yes, you need a plan. You don't have to make it an elaborate plan. Start with a simple plan. Writing, independently publishing and marketing your work is a journey. Know where you are starting and what you are starting with (skills, finance, contacts, etc.). Know where you are going (your destination, what you want to achieve and when). Know how you are going to get there (set long-term goals and short-term objectives.) Know how much time and money this journey will cost you, and what assistance you will need. A Business Plan is your road map (GPS) to your destination. Write a detailed business plan and follow it. Here is where to start:

Establish Your Business Legally

1. Give your business a name. Your business name may also be your imprint name. Use a fictitious Doing-Business-As-Name instead of your own name.

2. Identify your type of business. Is your business a sole proprietorship, general partnership or an LLC.?

3. Register your business

To complete steps 1-3 you will need to know how to name and register your business in your state (or country) of residence. This information is usually available on your state's website. If you are registering your business in New Jersey go to the State website http://www.nj.gov./njbusiness and click on the Business Portal. Here you will find all the information, forms, and the legal procedure for naming and registering your business in New Jersey.

Write Your Business Plan

Write out the details of your Business Plan. You may find this time consuming and challenging but you need to take the time to think it through and write down your thoughts. It is well worth the effort. Here is an outline you may follow or create your own:

A. Begin with an Overview (Executive Summary)

Describe your business. Include in this the type of business, ownership, location/physical address; dedicated business phone line, if available. Write answers to these questions:

- How are you running this business – full time or part-time?
- Will you be dedicating space in your home as office space solely for your business?
- Will you claim business use of your home on your income tax return?
- Hiring any help or going it alone?
- Looking to generate a personal income/ how much?
- How are you financing this business? What's your start-up capital, if any?
- What professional services will you need to purchase? (editor, cover designer, as needed) or will you be using pre-packaged publishing services?

B. List and describe your Products

- Will you be focusing on books only? What formats? (print, e-books, audio books). What's your genre?
- Will you offer any services, e.g. writing workshop ?

C. Set out your Financial Plan

- How are you financing your business.?
- What's your budget?

D. Set out your Writing Plan and Schedule

- What are you writing / When? Part-time or full time? set timelines. Include your daily writing schedule.

E. Identify Professional Services You May Need

- Editor?
- Tax advisor?
- Attorney?
- Accountant?
- Artist / Designer?
- Printing services / Self-publishing platform

F. What is your Production Plan?

- What will you produce and when? How many titles per year? Print books ? E-books? Audio books?

G. Set out Your Marketing Plan and Promotions

- Your primary target audience? Your core audience? Your secondary (or expanded) audience

H. List Your Resources

- Community, social media, writers organizations, etc.

You may not be able to input all of this information initially, but do as much as is feasible and review and modify your plan as your journey progresses.

Right now, you may want to focus only on this one book you are currently writing. It may not be your first book but it may be the first you are attempting to independently publish. Plan accordingly for this within the context of your over-all plan.

Action Item: My Business Plan

Using the above listed guidelines for creating a business plan

1. *Write the Executive Summary for your business plan*

_____
_____
_____
_____
_____
_____
_____
_____
_____

2. *Complete your business plan by answering the questions in Sections B – H of the business plan outline from the previous pages.*

_____
_____
_____
_____
_____
_____
_____
_____
_____
_____
_____
_____

CHAPTER FOUR

Are You Up to the Task?

The Publishing Process

There are numerous tasks involved in writing and publishing a book. Your goal as an independent author/publisher is to produce a book that looks good and meets professional publishing standards. You need to be in control of the process but you cannot do it all by yourself. You will need technical and professional help. How much you are able to do yourself, and how much support you will need depends on several factors.

Below I have listed most of the tasks that have to be completed at each stage of publication. Go through this list and make an honest and realistic assessment of what tasks, based on your level of commitment, your time availability, and your personal skill levels, you can do for yourself and how much professional support you may need.

It is important to the success of your writing business that you know, right from the start, what you can do effectively, and what tasks you must delegate to others. An honest self-assessment is key to your success as an independent author-publisher. Knowing your skills and limitations will save you a lot of time and eliminate frustrations. As the old saying goes, "don't bite off more than you can chew." Plan for the professional and technical support you need to successfully publish and market your book as an independent author/publisher.

Publishing and marketing your book is a big investment and any decision to obtain paid professional and technical support will impact your budget. But, on the other hand, there are also lots of free tools and services available to you. If you take time to do the research and learn to use these services, you will significantly reduce how much services you will need to purchase. Learning to use these tools will also significantly enhances your knowledge base and your author/publisher skills.

This task analysis will also help you to decide whether you want to do most of this work yourself and create your own publishing resource team to assist, as needed, or whether you want to purchase a package of services from a self-publishing services company, hand over your manuscript and your cash, and let the "self-publisher" do it while you raise more money to buy copies of your published book to sell.

Bottom line is, if you just want your book published without having to do the work yourself then independent publishing is not for you.

Task Analysis

Pre-Publication Stages

> - Decide on whether you are publishing a print book, e-book. Audio book or all of the above.
>
> - Decide on the publishing platform you will use. Your goal is to write and publish quality books economically and profitably. To avoid using and paying both the up-front cost and the after-cost of bundled self-publishing services you need to select a publishing platform such as CreateSpace, for example, that gives you free publishing support. Here you can publish your book free of cost. You also get the option purchase any additional professional service you need.
>
> - Decide on the trim size of your book and obtain or create appropriate templates. Many publishing and book printing

sites offer templates that you can download for free and save on your computer. You can either begin a new document or copy and paste your existing manuscript into the template To begin with, it is best to use a template generated by the publishing platform you chose as this is already formatted to their specification.

- ➤ Write, proofread and edit your manuscript.
- ➤ Choose an appropriate and effective title for your book.
- ➤ Write your book description (Back cover copy) and brief author bio.
- ➤ Obtain ISBN, LCCN (Library of Congress Control Number) Bookland EAN Barcode
- ➤ Get art work for cover design, and art work or illustration for book interior (if applicable)
- ➤ Understand Copyright basics and apply for Copyright registration
- ➤ Obtain permission (as needed) to use copyrighted material, photographs of others (even if you took the pictures yourself).
- ➤ Set up your website and if you are already using social media, continue to build a community of followers who share your interests and will generate interest in your work. If you are not using social media now is the time to begin to use this resource.

Publication Stage

- ➤ Select a publishing platform or POD printing service for print books, get quotes for your trim size, the number of copies you want to print, quality of paper and the binding style
- ➤ Select eBook format and publisher for your e-book
- ➤ Format your manuscript and design your interior book block.

- Create front matter such as copyright page, dedication, acknowledgement, table of contents and, if applicable, add back matter (bibliography, glossary, index, appendix).

- Design back and front cover and spine (available free or for a fee on CreateSpace).

- Convert your Word file to PDF and upload to your POD and/or e-book publisher.

- Upload your graphic file, as applicable, to POD or e-book publisher.

- Work on promotional campaign. Order promotional material.

- Plan your book launch.

- Receive and review proof copy . Edit as needed.

- Upload final copy and authorize printing.

- Order and pay for copies of finished books.

Post Production Stage

- Step-up your marketing campaign. Use social media.

- Prepare press release.

- Get reviews. Most independent author-publishers pay for these (e.g. Kirkus Review)

- Plan and execute book launch and follow-up promotional activities

- Update your website and create your online store to sell books from your website. Add links to resources for other writers and readers. Post short articles and other useful information on writing that others are free to use.

- Set up a PayPal account as a means of accepting credit cards from your website. Explore other credit card options

- Make sure your books are available to online bookstores. Register your title with Bowker Books In Print
- Seek to place your books in local community bookstores and libraries.

Record keeping , Sales Tax and income Tax Reporting

- Open a business bank account
- Create a spreadsheet to track your income from sales, etc., and your expenses
- Be prepared to handle sales tax reporting and income tax.

Assess. Evaluate. Prioritize

This is a formidable list of tasks, especially if this is your first venture into independent publishing. If you have previously published using a package of services from one of the many self-publishing service companies you may be thinking, not me! I'm just going to buy another package. On the other hand, if you have not published a book before, I can imagine you are thinking that you had better go find a publishing package. Don't.!

What you need to do now is prioritize. Decide exactly what you can do yourself, and what you must pay a professional to do. How much professional help you need depends on your own skill level and experience. How much you can afford will depend on your budget for this project. Go through this list again, this time with highlighters – one color for all you can comfortably do, another color for what you can do with minimal help, such as a free online tutorial.

What remains on the list are where you need the greatest amount of professional support. Now prioritize again. Which of these services will you pay a professional to do and which will you learn to do yourself? **Editing and a well-designed book cover are two things you should get professionally done, especially when you are just getting started in the independent publishing business.**

Most importantly, your choices at this stage should be determined by your vision and your goals as a successful independent author/publisher.

My Notes

CHAPTER FIVE

Create Your DIY Publishing Team

Whether you are a first time independent author/publisher or an experienced self-published author, your priority list must include

- ➢ Your choice of a publishing platform
- ➢ Professional Editorial Services
- ➢ Professional Design Services for interior and cover design.

Your independently published book needs to be professionally finished to the same high standard as those produced by traditional publishers. To achieve this you will need some support from professionals with experience in publishing. But instead of buying a pre-packaged bundle of services at exorbitant up-front cost you will create your own publishing support team and determine what services you need to purchase and what you can do for yourself.

Your book needs to be professionally edited and designed. You may be able to do most of this yourself but if your publishing business is a part time activity and you are juggling your time between writing, a full time job, and your numerous other life activities you will not be able to devote as much time as needed to thoroughly edit and lay out your book interior.

Additionally, your book cover needs to be professionally done. The cover is what will draw attention to your book and is one of your best sales tool.

Getting professional editorial and design support are the top priority selections you must make for your publishing project. A few clicks of the mouse will reveal a plethora of offerings for such services available on the Internet and you are bound to be confused as to what are your best choices.

> - Do you want to hand over your manuscript to a self-publishing service company and let them do it? No you've been there; done that!
>
> - Do you want to purchase only editorial and design services from an established publishing service company, do everything else yourself, and then upload your files to a print-on-demand only (POD) service?
>
> - Do you want to select a self-publishing service that will support your DIY effort by providing you with free DIY tools, and the option to purchase only the professional services you need?
>
> - Or should you hire individual industry professionals (free lancers) who are not affiliated with any self-publishing service company?

The choice is yours, but you want to be sure these are legitimate offerings and not scams. How do you know you are hiring a professional individual or a self-service publishing company with the integrity to deliver the quality of service you need and expect?

> - Do the research.
>
> - Read customers' reviews.
>
> - Ask questions and get recommendations.

If you decide to hire a free-lance professional editor and book designer for your project, get references and samples of their work. You should also have a formal contract or written agreement, with appropriate signatures, cost, terms and conditions of the services. Be specific about the services you need. Know what you are getting.

Selecting A Publishing Service

Before you select a publishing service

- ➤ Review your publishing goals, your production plan, your marketing plan, and your vision for your publishing business.

- ➤ Decide whether you want print services only, eBook services only, or print book, eBook, and distribution services.

- ➤ Do an internet search for publishers (not vanity publishers) who offer the services you need and carefully evaluate what they are offering. Read posted customers' reviews. Get word-of-mouth recommendation from other independent publishers who have used these services.

Print Services Only (POD)

This is primarily a book printing service. To use this service all parts of your book must be camera ready and you are purchasing only binding and printing services. I will refer to these as book manufacturers.

In preparing to write this I checked out several book manufacturing companies who offer print-on-demand only services and I will summarize here what 48-HourBooks offers. I choose 48HourBooks also because my daughter has used this service for one of her books and this company delivered what it offered, in a timely manner, and the finished product was good. Also this company gets very good reviews form their customers.

When you upload your camera-ready book files to 48HourBooks they will print and bind your book. How much this POD only service will cost you varies with the number of books you choose to print. You can log into 48HourBooks website and get an instant quote for the number of books you want to be printed.

To get an instant quote you select the trim size of your book, the binding style, the interior in black & white or color, and the cover type. Input your production time and your zip code to calculate the cost. On an order of 100 books you get an additional 25 books free.

48-HourBooks also offers some author support services such as

- ➤ Free download of their template for formatting your manuscript
- ➤ Create-a-cover service. ($100.00) or free if you already have a cover file
- ➤ ISBN & Barcode ($125.00) if you do not have your own.
- ➤ Printed Proof ($40.00)
- ➤ Free PDF proof

This information is provided primarily as an example of POD only services that are available to you. The figures quoted were current at the time of writing. It is your responsibility, not only to verify this information if you choose to use this service, but also to research and compare other POD book manufacturers (Lulu, the Book Patch, Book Print On Demand) and a host of others as an online search will reveal.. Choose one that best meets your needs for print service only.

What are the advantages and disadvantages of using a book manufacturer for book printing service (POD) ?

You can print as many or as few books as you need. For some POD service providers your cost per book remains the same whether you print one or more. Others offer you incentives to order in bulk by either reducing the cost per book or throwing in a number of additional copies. Whether you order your print book one at a time or in bulk, you still have to resolve the matter of distribution and marketing. How do you get your book beyond your local readers?

Print and Distribution Services

Two excellent publishing platform for print and distribution services are

- ➤ CreateSpace, offered by Amazon

> IngramSpark/Lightning Source

There are others that offer print and distribution services but these two are my recommended publishing platforms of choice for the author/publisher. If you are truly serious about taking full control of the process and proceeds of your writing business, then these are excellent publishing platforms to explore. You can publish and distribute your books free of cost on CreateSpace and for a minimal set-up fee on IngramSpark You may also consider Lulu which offers a wide range of formats, including photo books, calendars, and a platform specially designed for kids who write. As previously stated, all choices are predicated on the type of book you are publishing, your vision for your book and your goals as an independent author/publisher. Bottom line is, with the advance of technology, there are more and more resources being made available to you the independent author/publisher to succeed at self-publishing. No longer do you need to suffer from rejections by traditional publishers, pay "vanity publishers/self-publishers" to publish your book, or do it all by yourself.

IngramSpark Self-Publishing Platform

IngramSpark is part of the Ingram Book Group which is the largest distributor of books in print as well as in digital content. Ingram Book Group distribution service is worldwide and includes wholesalers, retailers, book stores, libraries and universities, as well as all digital devices. Ingram Spark/Lightning Source offers printing and distribution services to independent authors and publishers. However, if you are not already working with this publishing platform Lightning Source may not be available to you, the self-publisher.

To use IngramSpark go to http://ingramspark.com/portal/HowItworks

and set up an account. There is a $49.00 title set-up fee for print book only or for both print book and e-book if you want these publish simultaneously. The $49.00 is refunded to you with an initial purchase of 50 print books. For E-book the set up fee is $25.00.

To set up an account you will need to input your contact and banking information, your ISBN. You must purchase your own ISBN. Upload your print book and your e-book files, and IngramSpark will print and distribute your book locally and internationally. As an independent author/publisher you need to explore and use the services IngramSpark offers. IngramSpark gets percentage of revenue from their sale of your book through its distribution service. Details are available on the website.

CreateSpace Self-Publishing Platform

CreateSpace is the self-publishing platform offered by Amazon. This is easily the one-stop shop for all you need to create, publish and market your books. To access the services provided by CreateSpace go to http://www.createspace.com and create an account. After you have set up your account, take some time to explore the site. It's user-friendly and easy to navigate. If you need help, that is readily available either from a live representative or its online chat system.

CreateSpace DIY Services

CreateSpace offers free tools that you, the independent author, can use for a totally DIY publishing experience. You can use the **Interior Reviewer** to help format your book file, and to catch and correct any formatting errors before your book goes to print. You can use the **Cover Creator** to design and create you own DIY book cover.

Here is a summary of how this works. For full details go http://www.createspace.com

The Interior Reviewer

To use the Interior Reviewer, upload your Word.doc or pdf file and the Interior Reviewer automatically changes it into a print ready document. Interior Reviewer also scans and highlights any formatting issues so these can be easily located and fixed. You can then review and proof read a virtual version of your book online or order a print proof. If your file is not formatted to match your trim size Interior Reviewer can automatically fix that. For, example, your file is formatted as letter size, but your book trim size is 6x9 trade paperback, Interior Reviewer will auto-scale your file to the desired size.

Cover Creator

Cover Creator offers several designs, themes and colors for your book cover. You input your own images and text to format the cover you want. If you do not have the image you need for your cover you can select one from Creative Space gallery free of charge.

With CreateSpace DIY service there is no set up fee. You get good support and immediate response to your questions. Additionally, there is an online chat system for instant help.

CreateSpace will give you a free ISBN but CreateSpace must be listed as your publisher. Depending on your vision for your writing business you may want to use your own.

CreateSpace Professional Services

The site also offers professional editorial, design and marketing services for a fee. The beauty of this is that the services are not bundled at all. You can buy none. You can buy one or you can buy all, depending on your needs and budget. You have total control of the choices you make for your book design and publication.

Check out the offers for editorial services, interior designs and, cover designs at http://www.createspace.com

How do these play out in terms of your budget? Again, prioritize. Purchase only what you need. You will have to do the work but the rewards are much greater.

CreateSpace Distribution Services

All CreateSpace titles are distributed through Amazon. CreateSpace offers you your own eStore and make your book available to Amazon Kindle, Amazon.com, Amazon Europe, and an expanded distribution option that places your book in other online book stores and retailers throughout USA. CreateSpace does not distribute your book worldwide. For worldwide distribution CreateSpace sends your book to Ingram.

As an independent author/publisher you need both IngramSpark and CreateSpace publishing platforms. Go to their websites and spend some time exploring what each has to offer. You should also read what other indie authors are saying about both publishing platforms.

Cost of Publishing, Book Pricing, and Royalty

If you do not purchase any of the editorial or design services offered by CreateSpace, publishing your book on CreateSpace is free. Each time CreateSpace fulfills a purchase order for one or more of your books through one of its sales channel CreateSpace get a percentage of the list price which you set for your book. When your book is sold through Amazon.com or Amazon Europe CreateSpace gets 40% of the list price. When you sell through CreateSpace eStore CreateSpace get 20% of the list price. For expanded distribution CreateSpace gets 60%. To calculate your royalty and publishing cost you subtract from the list price the sales channel percentage plus the fixed charges (based on page count and whether your book has black and white or full color interior) plus the per page charge. The difference is your royalty.

For specific examples of book pricing and royalty calculation go to the website.

Buying Copies of Your Book

You make author purchase of your books through your CreateSpace account. The cost of a proof copy is the same as the cost of a single book, plus shipping and handling. Sales tax may apply. You pay for your purchase at the time of ordering. There is no royalty earned on author purchases.

My Notes

CHAPTER SIX

Buy and Use Your Own ISBN and Barcode

Each edition and each format of your book is unique and must have its own identifier. That is, if you publish your book in hard cover, soft cover and e-book format each of these must be identified separately. Each must have its own ISBN if you intend to sell your books through wholesale and retail channels.

ISBN - International Standard Book Number

ISBN is a worldwide identification system used to identify each book and avoid errors in the distribution of books. When you buy ISBNs and register your books on www.myindetifiers.com your book information will be stored in Books In Print database and your title made available to retailers, libraries, online book stores, and others in the book distribution and marketing business. **R.R. Bowker** is the International Standard Book Numbering Agency. Purchase the ISBNs you need for your books at https://www.myidentifiers.com/isbn/main

One ISBN costs $125.00. A packet of 10 costs $295.00. If you plan to publish your book in more than one format then it is best to buy 10 ISBNs

You will notice that there are other places - "authorized agents" - that offer ISBN and barcode packages – some at much lower cost than Bowker's. Some of these "authorized agents" are marketing directly to self-publishers. My advice is that you go directly to http://myidentifiers.com to purchase your ISBN & BooklandEAN Barcodes from Bowker.

You may choose, later on in your publishing journey, to buy from these other sources because of the cost saving. It's your choice but – a word of caution especially to new authors and those of us who are on a tight publishing budget - Don't be deceived. You need to verify that these agents are legitimate and your information with them is secure. You want to be sure that your book is registered properly.

BARCODES

There are several Barcode systems in the USA. For your book you need the Bookland EAN/13 with add-on. This is the standard barcode for books.

Barcodes are placed on the back cover of your book with the ISBN. Barcodes identify pricing information and are required by most wholesale and retailers. You must have an ISBN to get a barcode.

You can purchase Bookland EAN (European Article Number) Barcodes at http://www.myidentifiers.com when you buy your ISBN. The current price is $25.00.

The Barcode is a scanable graphic representation of your ISBN. It encodes your book title and your book retail price. Your book ISBN is always printed above the barcode.

Price Add-on: On most books there are two sets of barcodes side by side. The larger one on the left is derived from the ISBN. The smaller one on the right is the 5-degits price add-on. The first digit tells you what currency is being used and the other four digits identify the price of your book. For the USA the first digit is a 5. So if it is 51675 that means the price of the book is $16.75 (USA). This price add-on is required on all your books.

ISBN: Why You Need Your Own ISBN

Your ISBN identifies you as the publisher of your book (i.e. your publishing company as your imprint if you have registered your writing business and are using a doing-business-as-Name).

If you use an ISBN (for free or purchased) that was issued to another publisher that publisher becomes the imprint of record for your book.

Here is an example. If you use CreateSpace Self-Publishing Platform for your books CreateSpace offers four ISBN options. You can have a free ISBN. You can purchase an ISBN for $10.00 or $99.00 or you can use your own. This is good for your budget! However, the choice you make should be determined by your goals and vision as an independent publisher.

If you choose the free ISBN CreateSpace is listed as the publisher of your book. Your book will be printed and distributed with CreateSpace Self-Publishing Platform as your imprint of record. You can use this ISBN only with CreateSpace. You can sell your book through all of CreateSpace distribution channels but you cannot use any other distributor.

With the $10.00 option you get to choose your publishing platform, that is, you can list your company (your own imprint) as imprint of record. CreateSpace will print and distribute your book through all its local distribution channels and some of its expanded distribution channels. You cannot use this ISBN with another publisher / distributor. You can use it only with the CreateSpace Self-Publishing Platform.

When you purchase the $99.00 Custom ISBN from CreateSpace you use your publishing company as the imprint of record and you can use this ISBN with any publisher. You can sell through all CreateSpace standard distribution channels and some of its expanded distribution channels but if you also want to publish your book with IngramSpark you should opt out of CreateSpace expanded distribution. CreateSpace sends your title to Ingram Book Group for worldwide distribution.

If you register for CreateSpace expanded distribution you cannot use this same ISBN with IngramSpark publishing platform. You will need to buy another ISBN for your book as this one that you purchased from CreateSpace will already be in their system.

With all of the above three options CreateSpace will register your book ISBN information with Bowker Books In Print.

When you use your own ISBN (purchased from Bowker) you are the publisher of record.. CreateSpace will print and distribute your books but you must register your book with Bowker Books In Print. You can also use your own ISBN to publish with IngramSpark and elsewhere.

If you are publishing an e-book and print book you will need two ISBN – one for each format. If you later decide to revise and publish a different edition of your book you will also need separate ISBN for each edition.

My Notes

REGISTER YOUR BOOK TITLE

Books In Print by Bowker

As an independent author/publisher you must register your book with Books In Print by Bowker if you want your book to be found worldwide. Books In Print is defined as "the leading bibliographic database for libraries, publishers and retailers around the world." When you register your book with Books In Print by Bowker your book becomes a part of this huge bibliographic database, visible and accessible to everyone who is looking to purchase publications.

How to Register Your Book

Wait until your book is published and ready for sale then you submit the title information for the assigned ISBN.

When you purchased your ISBN from Bowker you created an account. This account has a list of your ISBN. Log into http://myidentifer.com and access your account and follow the directions carefully

- ➢ Select Manage ISBN (List of used and unused ISBN will appear).
- ➢ Access the Title Form
- ➢ Click on the ISBN for the book you are registering and click Assign Title
- ➢ Fill out Title Information Form (title & cover, contributor (author), format and trim size. (List size in decimal), pricing
- ➢ Click Submit
- ➢ Upload the book image
- ➢ Upload full text in pdf format. Identify your pdf file by the ISBN assigned to your book.

For complete details and step-by-step instructions, before you begin the title registration, download and read these articles provided by Bowker.

ISBN Guides- Basic Information and *Title Set Up Registration*
You will find the link to these on http://myidentifier.com

My Notes

CHAPTER SEVEN

Turn Your Manuscript Into A Published Book

In the preceding chapters we covered a lot of information intended to give you a basic understanding of what is involved in self-publishing, how to ditch self-publishing service packages and set up your independent publishing business, and how to publish successfully using free online tools and limited paid professional services.

Your Manuscript versus Print-Ready Files

If you are a first time author or a published author who has used only the prepackaged services offered by self-publishing service companies then, most likely, you have a Word document formatted to standard manuscript size which is 8.5x11.00 page size, double spaced text with one-inch margin on all sides.

To prepare print-ready files you will need to change the page size, margin, and line spacing. Before you attempt to set up this on your own, access the publishing platform you have chosen for your book and read its formatting requirement. Each print-on-demand publisher has its own unique model and specific printing requirements. Your file must be formatted to satisfy these requirements or it will be rejected. Fortunately, you can access and use free template formatted for your book trim size which will save you a lot of time and effort.

Select a Trim Size

Go to your publisher's website and select a trim size for your book. Trim Size is the final size of your book after it is printed, bound and trimmed. Standard size of trade paperback is 6"x 9". Some publishers offer more choices than others. At IngramSpark, for example, you will find a much wider offering of trim sizes than at CreateSpace. You will choose the trim size most suited to the type of book you are publishing. For distribution purposes, the size you choose to make your book must meet industry standard. This book you are reading is 6"x9" trade paperback., perfect bound.

Select A Template for Interior Pages

Your interior pages must be formatted to the trim size you selected. Publishing platforms that support DIY author-publishers have free templates for your trim size that you can use. Select a template for your trim size, download and save it on your computer. Copy and paste your manuscript into the template. If it is a huge file you may want to do this by sections or chapters. Save it with an appropriate file name for your book interior. Read through and check for accuracy. Edit as needed.

Be careful to remove all the filler-text that your publisher inserted in the header, footer and body of the template. The purpose of filer-text in the template is to guide you as you work with the template. You do not want these to show up in your published work.

Save the template on your computer, and when you are ready to begin your next book use the template.

Using a professionally formatted template for your book interior is a great time saver and simplifies what can be a really frustrating task for an inexperienced author/publisher.

Parts of Your Book Interior (Your Book Block)

Your book interior (your book block) has three distinct parts. These are the Front Matter, the Book Block Text Matter, and the Back Matter. Your book interior file must contain all three sections combined in the correct format as a single document. The template you downloaded from your publisher's website will have allocated pages for all three sections.

Front Matter

These are the pages that appear before the main text and serve to introduce your book to the readers. Which of the following front matter pages you will need depend on whether your book is fiction or non-fiction. Here are the type of pages that is appropriate as front matter, and the sequence in which they should occur in your print book.

- **Half Title Page**. This is the first page of your book and contains the title only. Do not include byline or subtitle on this page.
- **Series Title Page** is for listing your previously published work, in chronological order. You may begin with the phrase, "also by (Your Name).
- **Title Page** has the full title, sub-title (if any), author's name, imprint and location. If you have purchased and are using your own ISBN you are the publisher of record so use your business or imprint name.
- **Copyright Page**: See page 20 for details of copyright page.
- **Dedication**, that is, a tribute to someone who has impact your life or your writing.
- **Table of Content** used mainly for nonfiction books. However, if your fiction book is divided into chapters and each chapter has a unique title you may include a content page.
- **Acknowledgement** expresses note of appreciation to those who have helped and/or supported your work in any way.
- **Foreword** is a statement, mainly in a nonfiction book, written by someone other than the author who is an expert in a relevant field.
- **Preface,** in nonfiction books, tells why you wrote the book.

Book Block Text (Main Text)

This is the main part of your manuscript. It may contain an introduction, the main body of work that you have spent all those long hours creating and, a conclusion or epilogue.

A formal introductory section and a summary type conclusion are more likely to be included in nonfiction work. Work of fiction such as novels are divided into chapters with or without unique chapter headings.

The Introduction highlights a feature of the main text or the overall concept of the work that you want to bring to your readers' attention prior to their reading the book. If you have included charts, diagrams, questions, space for notes, you may want to include instructions in the introduction on how these should be used.

The Epilogue is a brief concluding section, primarily in a work of fiction, which speaks directly to the readers. It may be a brief "look ahead" or continuation of the story years later or it may be an update about the characters whereabouts

The Conclusion summarizes the key points, concepts ideas and /or advice presented throughout the book, and should leave the readers with a clear understanding of the concepts presented and some guidelines on how to use this information.

Back Matter includes appendix, notes, index, glossary, resources and a bibliography or list of references. You may also include an Order Form for purchase of your book and a 'sneak preview" of your next book.

Putting it All Together

Your next step is to put all the parts of your book interior together in the correct sequence. If you are using a template made to your publishers' submission specification you just need to copy and place your text in the appropriate sections. You don't have to worry about page size and margins. Those are already set for you. If, however, your book contains charts and diagrams, images and other objects you should get some professional help with the graphics. If it's all plain text, you can just paste that into the template, section or chapter by chapter. Better yet, if you had created your text from the beginning using the template then you just need to check to ensure that all text is in its proper place, that there are no blank right-hand pages, no page numbers on the front matter pages, and that you have removed all the guide text your publisher inserted in the template.

Create a PDF

When you are satisfied that your Word.doc is complete and accurate you can create a PDF. You should download your publisher's instructions and specifications for creating and submitting PDF.

However, if you are working with CreateSpace as your publishing platform, my recommendation is that, at this point, you should use CreateSpace Internal Reviewer to review your internal file. Upload your Word.doc and

Interior Reviewer will convert it to a print ready format. This is an easier, faster, and more accurate way of getting your file ready for publishing.

Create Your Book Cover

We all say, "A picture is worth a thousand words." How much is your book cover worth in terms of book sales? Your book cover is not just there to protect and keep the pages of your book together. Your book cover reflects the content of your book and is one of your most powerful marketing tool. So, don't skimp on your book cover.

Your book cover introduces your book to the readers. It is responsible for creating the first impression any reader will get of your book, and as the saying goes, first impressions are lasting impressions. Your book cover will make or break a sale! So don't skimp on your book cover. Although you have tools available to help you build your DIY book cover, you may want to use the services of a professional cover designer instead.

Before you do a "blind' search for book cover design service, first check your DIY publisher to ascertain what cover design services, if any, are offered. If you are using CreateSpace Self-Publishing you have several options. You can use its Cover Creator to assist you in the layout and formatting of your cover at no cost to you, upload your fully designed camera ready cover, or you can use its professional services for a fee.

If you are able to create your own cover PDF file but need some professional support to make sure it meets your publisher's submission requirements, you have the options of using CreateSpace Supported Cover PDF service for a fee of $99.00. For this fee CreateSpace will review your file, make necessary adjustments and fix any problems with your original. You will then get a revised digital file to review and approve. If this option does not meet your need CreateSpace offers a Custom Cover for $399.00 and a Custom Cover Premier for $599.00. For detail go to www.createspace.com.

Whether you choose to pay to have your book cover designed or do it yourself will be determined by your vision and goal for your book.

The Front Cover and Spine

The Front cover and the spine announce the book title and author. The spine may also display the publisher's logo. The front cover may also display images or illustrations reflecting the content of the book.

The Back Cover

I cannot overstate the importance of your book's back cover. Whereas the front cover captures the reader's attention, it is the function of the back cover to hook and compel the reader to buy your book.. Your back cover copy or book blurb is your sales pitch. In 250 – 300 words you need to write a brief description of your book, capturing the essence of what your book is about and why the reader should buy your book.

This is not so easy to do. But you know your book better than anyone else and you know why you wrote it and how it will benefit your readers. You want to emphasize the benefit. Start with a leading question or statement that resonate with your readers; something that will affect or appeal to the reader in a personal or emotional way. Follow up with a bulleted list of benefits to be derived from the content of your non-fiction book. For fiction you may include few lines of plot, allude to the conflict and question the resolution, or add an intriguing snippet of dialogue -- anything that will pique the readers interest and make him/her desire to know more.

If you have endorsements from experts in your field, or reviews, you can also use excerpts from these on your back cover

Author Photo and Bio

Use a small photo and add a short bio. Include what qualifies you to write the book.

ISBN and Barcode
Be sure to include this in the lower right section of your back cover.

My Notes:

_____
_____
_____
_____

CHAPTER EIGHT

Polish Before You Publish

Genre-specific Self-editing and Editorial Evaluation of Your Manuscript

You are almost ready to publish. You have finished writing your book. Your book interior file is laid out and well formatted, and your cover file is also ready to go. Now what? Take the following steps to self-edit and evaluate your book block and book cover

Self-Editing Your Book Files

- First put your files away. Take a break. Clear your mind. Focus on something else. Do this for at least a week and then return to your book. While you are "clearing your head" you may ask someone you trust to read through your manuscript.
- Using your computer software run a complete spelling and grammar check, and edit as indicated. When in doubt, refer to the *Chicago Manual of Style* as your editorial guide.
- Print your complete interior file and read through your book from start to finish.

First Reading

This read-through is primarily to assess readability, fluency and general appeal. Do this as a reader and not as the author. If you didn't write it would you really read it? Keep a highlighter and a post-it pad handy. As you read through, highlight any error that catches your attention and flag any paragraph that is not clear or does not flow well, but do not make changes now.

Follow-up on First Reading

Go back to your computer, go through your text, correct any errors you highlighted and fix any section you flagged during the first reading. Consider any feedback you got from the person you asked to read your manuscript. Edit your manuscript. Cut, re-arrange or rewrite as appropriate. Do another grammar and spelling check using your computer software. Print your book file again and sit in for your second read-through.

Second Reading

Make this reading genre-specific. Is your book fiction or non-fiction? You will focus on elements of non-fiction or fiction. If you are asking a colleague or critique ask for an evaluation of sections of your book using the question listed below. Your objective here is to evaluate your book using genre-specific criteria. In light of your answers and the responses you receive from your colleague or critique group, is your book ready for publication or does it need more work? If it does, can you do this or do you need professional editorial service?

Self-Editing Your Non-fiction Manuscript

How effective is your opening?
- ➢ Do the introduction and preface help the reader understand the unique nature of your book and your reason and qualification for writing it?
- ➢ Is the opening material sufficient to interest the reader?
- ➢ Does the introduction or first chapter set up the basis for the rest of the book?
- ➢ Does the first page grab the reader's attention and compel him to keep reading?
- ➢ Does the author (you) establish a strong voice in the first few pages?

Are the structure, organization and language appropriate for the content of your book?.
- ➢ Is your message clear?

- Do paragraphs develop logically with a central idea and supportive details.
- Do they flow naturally into each other?
- Are they effective? That is, do they function as intended? Narrative paragraphs tell a story in sequence. Logical sequence paragraphs are for logical development of ideas. Explanatory paragraphs provide support for your message by supplying facts, quotes, and illustrations. Descriptive paragraphs create mood, set scenes, describe setting (place and situation).
- Are the general facts and information accurate and consistent throughout?
- Are these supported by appropriate documentation, if necessary?
- Is the general structure well organized with a natural, logical, and cohesive progression of ideas, observations, or events?
- Is the book divided into sections or chapters with appropriate titles and/or sub-headings?
- Are these divisions presented in an attractive, consistent and professional manner?
- Is there a table of contents?
- Does the table of contents reflect the exact chapter titles and organization of the book?
- Are titles and sub-headings interesting, enticing, and descriptive?
- Does the last chapter or section provide an appropriate closure for the subject matter of your book?

Are your sentences within each paragraph well-crafted?
Sentences and paragraphs are your building blocks. Carefully and creatively used they create your masterpiece.
- Do they vary in length and type with the emphasis in the right place for effect and clarity?
- Are they free of stylistic errors such as fragments, repetition or use of passive voice?
- Is the use of language (word choice and sentence structure) appropriate for the genre? And for your audience?

Are the basic premise and tone appropriate?
- Have you set a tone that is appropriate for the genre?
- Is this consistent throughout the book?
- Is the basic premise of the book appealing?
- Is this consistent throughout?

Is the Back Matter accurate, appropriate and functional?
- ➢ Does your content need notes to clarify, amplify or document specific passages throughout the text?
- ➢ If so, have you arranged the notes by chapter in a note section?
- ➢ Do you need a glossary for unusual words and phrases?
- ➢ If so, are the words with their definitions listed alphabetically?
- ➢ Have you included list of resources valuable to the readers?
- ➢ Have you included any marketing tools? Order Form? Blurbs of your previously published or coming-soon titles?
- ➢ Is there a link to your website or Facebook group?
- ➢ Is there a call to action? Special offers?

My Notes

Self-Editing Your Fiction Manuscript
(A Novel)

Does your manuscript have all the basic elements of fiction?

The Opening Chapter
- Does your book begin with a bang or a whimper? Your opening is important. It must hook the reader and compel him to continue reading.
- Does the opening chapter introduce the protagonist effectively?
- Does it establish the tone for your book?

The Theme
- Is the theme or focus clear?
- Does the focus/theme remain clear and consistent as the plot develops? (exposition, rising action, climax and resolution)

Structure
- Does it have a well-defined arc: beginning, middle and ending?

The Plot
- Does the plot move forward throughout the manuscript with no obvious holes in the storyline?
- Is the action driven by struggle between opposing forces?
- Are all incidents related to the plot and relevant to the story?
- Is the pace appropriate?
- Are there turning points in the plot and situations that heighten the conflict?

Setting
- Is the setting appropriate for the story?
- Does it provide a sense of place to the plot?
- Does it add to the mood or evoke emotional tension?

Characters
- Are characters realistic, believable, well rounded or flat?
- Do they have flaws, personal agendas, motivation and goals?
- Is the protagonist and/or antagonist highly motivated?
- Is there adequate struggle/obstacles/tension within and between characters?
- Is there character growth?
- Has the main character changed in any way by the end of the story?

Dialogue
- Is the dialogue conversational and easy to follow?
- Does the dialogue reveal character traits?
- Is there a good balance of dialogue and action?
- Is the dialogue used effectively?
- Does it help to move the plot along?
- Is the dialogue punctuated correctly?

Point of View
- Is the point of view clearly defined?
- Is it maintained consistently throughout?
- Is there any problem with shifting of point of view throughout the novel?

Ending/Resolution
- Is the ending satisfying to the reader?
- Is it appropriate for the story?

My Notes

_____
_____
_____
_____
_____
_____
_____
_____
_____
_____
_____
_____
_____
_____
_____
_____
_____
_____
_____

Self-Editing Your Book Cover

You have a fully formatted cover that you have either paid a professional cover designer to create or you did it yourself.
- Is it a single one-piece PDF that includes the front cover, the back cover, and the spine?
- Is it the same trim size as your book?
- Does the spine contain the book title, author, and your imprint logo (if applicable?).

Asses and Edit Your Front Cover
- Does the title reflect the content of the book?
- Is there a subtitle?
- Does the subtitle amplify or clarify the title?
- Are spelling, grammar, and punctuation of the subtitle correct?
- Is your choice of fonts appropriate?
- Is your front cover image (if any) captivating and appropriate for your genre?

Assess and edit your marketing text
- Is the back cover copy (synopsis/marketing text) appealing?
- Does it provide enough detail to capture the potential reader's interest?
- Is the pitch strong enough to entice the reader into buying your book?
- Is the category for the back cover correct
- Are the BISAC codes appropriate ?
- Do you have an ISBN and barcode for this title?

Assess and Edit Author Credentials
- Have you included what uniquely qualifies you to write the book? Is this convincing?
- Does it demonstrate credibility in the subject area?

My Notes

CHAPTER NINE

Ready to Publish

You have thoroughly assessed and edited all segments of your book using the questions in the previous chapter as your guide. You have shared sections of your book with your writers' association, your critique group, family member, colleague or writing partner and have received their feedback. Are you satisfied that your book is ready for publication or does it need more work? If it does need more work, is this what you can fix yourself with the assistance of free online tools like the Interior Reviewer provided by CreateSpace or do you need some professional editorial and design help?

No matter how thorough you are or how well-equipped in knowledge and writing skills or how many times you have gone through your text it is still likely that you have missed something. So, my recommendation is that you get technical support or a professional pair of eyes to look at your book before you release it to the world.

In a previous chapter I made reference to CreateSpace provided by Amazon as an excellent self-publishing platform for the do-it-yourself independent authors. If you have chosen to use this publishing platform and have already set up an account you can now utilize either the free tools or the paid editorial and design services offered.

Your Book Cover
Starting from Scratch Using CreateSpace Free Tools

CreateSpace offers you technical support for your DIY cover. So if you do not have a fully formatted cover but you have all your cover text, your artwork, ISBN and barcode you can build your own cover using CreateSpace Cover Creator. This tool will format and size your cover automatically while you do the layout, design and marketing copy for your book. To use the Cover Creator log in to CreateSpace website and read the information and instructions on how to use this tool. Go to your member dashboard to start the project and launch Cover Creator. Follow the instructions for building your cover. If you do not have artwork or your own ISBN you can choose an image from CreateSpace gallery, and you can also get a free ISBN or purchase one from CreateSpace. See details on CreateSpace website or chapter seven of this book.

Starting with a Fully Formatted Cover

If you already have a fully formatted cover done by you using your own software program such as Adobe Photoshop® or you have paid a professional designer for this check to make sure it meets CreateSpace specification and follow the submission instructions.

Using CreateSpace Professional Design Services

CreateSpace offers its authors a Custom Cover and a Custom Cover Premier. The service cost $399.00 and $599.00 respectively. If you want to use this service check out the details on CreateSpace website.

My Notes

_____
_____
_____
_____
_____
_____
_____
_____
_____
_____
_____
_____

Your Book Interior

Using CreateSpace Free Tools

- ➢ Select the Interior Reviewer.
- ➢ Read the Interior Reviewer Guide to understand what this tool does and what you will have to do.
- ➢ Upload your Word.doc or PDF file and the Interior Reviewer will automatically convert your file into a print ready document.
- ➢ Interior Reviewer will scan and highlight any formatting problem so you can fix these online.
- ➢ You will also get a virtual version of your book so you can preview and proofread it online. Or you can order a print proof at the cost of printing only.
- ➢ Proofread your print copy and make any corrections necessary. You can then upload your edited version, and if this is your final perfect version, approve publication.

Ordering a print proof of your book will give you an opportunity to see and examine your book as it will appear on the market, and you can decide on whether you need to make any changes or approve your book , as is, for publication.

Using Professional Editorial Services

Professional editorial service is expensive. How much you will pay to edit your book varies with the number of pages your book contains and the level of editing it requires. A standard page count is 250 words. Copyediting at one cent per word is $2.50 per page. Different editors use different terminology to identify what they do. So if you are purchasing editorial service be sure to ascertain exactly what tasks your editor associates with each term. This is important because if you purchase copyediting the tasks the editor offers as copyediting is all you will get and that may not be what you need most.

For the purpose of this text and for my practice as an editor, **copyediting** is similar to proof reading. The focus here is on grammatical details (accuracy and consistency in use of tense, subject-verb agreement, pronoun reference, etc), spelling, and punctuation. **Line editing** provides all of the above plus suggestions on how to improve the sentence structure and paragraph flow, plot, characterization. **Developmental editing** focuses on improving the overall content and structure of your manuscript to publication standard.

Using CreateSpace Professional Editorial Service.

CreateSpace offers four levels of editorial services beginning with the lowest level of editing for $160.00 for the first 10,000 words, followed by a per word cost for each word above 10,000 words. For details and the cost of other levels of editing go to CreateSpace website.

Totally Free Publishing

Publishing your print book on CreateSpace is totally free. There is no set up fee and you are not required to purchase any of the professional for-a-fee services that are offered. So, as soon as you are confident that your book is perfect and ready for publication go ahead, upload your file. CreateSpace Internal reviewer will check your file and if there is no problem with format, etc, CreateSpace will create a virtual copy of your book for your preview. A pdf version and a print version of your book proof will be made available to you. Download the pdf version and order a print version. The print version shows what your published book will be like. Proof read and edit and re-submit your file if needed. Otherwise, authorize publication. One advantage of publishing with CreateSpace is that you can have your paperback book converted to an eBook for Kindle.

Kindle Conversion Service

When you use Kindle conversion Service your e-book will be available worldwide. All elements of your paperback book will become available on any Amazon Kindle reading device and on all Kindle Apps.

- ➢ Purchase the conversion service for $79.00
- ➢ Create an account with Kindle Direct Publishing at kdp.amazon.com
- ➢ Give CreateSpace your email address for your KDP account
- ➢ CreateSpace will set up your title information and upload your file to Kindle Direct Publishing (KDP)

CHAPTER TEN

Publish and Publicize Your Book

Your book is published. Congratulations! You have worked hard to get to this point. You have spent many long hours writing, reading, researching, rewriting and editing. You are exhausted but doesn't it feel good that your bank account is not depleted from paying big upfront cost to publish your book and to buy copies of your book for marketing? So go ahead and celebrate!

Publishing your book is a commendable achievement but it is not the final step of your publishing journey. It is a significant milestone along the way. Your next big challenge now is to publicize and market your book. With this in mind, your first thought may be social media and social networking. That's good if you have been building a social media network and are competent and confident with using this medium to publicize your book and promote sale. Otherwise you can waste a lot of time on social media.

I know that not every author reading this book has such a large social media following. Maybe, it's because that's not what you do best or maybe it does not interest you, or you just did not have the time in the past to devote to building a social media profile and a following. Now is as good a time as ever to explore how to use social media to promote your book.

When you use CreateSpace as your publishing platform your print book and your e-book are immediately available on Amazon.com and through CreateSpace other distribution channels. When you publish with IngramSpark, and when you register your title with Bowker Books In Print your title becomes immediately available to anyone who is searching for publication, so with these resources it is no longer a question of how to make your book available to readers. It's a matter of your letting readers know your book is readily available.

The Social Media Approach

Use social media to create a buzz about your book and to spread the word to and through your friends, family members, colleagues and all your other contacts on Facebook, Twitter, LinkedIn, Pinterest, and wherever you have an account. But how do you use these media to spread the word? Here are some online sites that share excellent ideas on how to harness and use this powerful tool. You do not have to reproduce these ideas. Just reading and following some of the advice you find on these sites will stimulate your own creativity and trigger ideas of your own which you in turn, I hope, will share with other authors.

http://www.socialmediaexaminer.com
Michael Stelzner offers "9 Ways to Use Social Media to Launch a Book.

http://bookmarketingmaven.com

http://selfpublishingnews.com

www.shelleyhitz.com
Here you will also find links to excellent resources for the Christian writer.

http://www.goodreads.com
Join Goodreads author program and promote your book for free.

My Notes:

_____
_____
_____
_____
_____
_____
_____
_____

The Conventional or Traditional Approach

Not everyone uses social media and there are many readers who will not purchase a book online. As a writer you want to make use of social media and online tools to promote your book but you cannot disregard the tried and proven conventional ways.

Throw an At-Home Launch Party.

This one is for your friends, neighbors, family members, colleagues, local community leaders. They know you personally and are proud of your achievement. Not only will they buy your book for themselves; they will buy copies as gifts for their friends and family members. I have had much success with book sales at this type of book event. I have a friend who repeatedly buys at least ten copies of my books which she sends out to her friends, colleagues, and family members, with little notes telling them why they should read this book. Some she gives away as gifts and sometimes the recipients will pay her for the books. Others spread the word and take book orders from their friends.

At-Home Launch parties can be very successful especially if the theme or message resonates with the audience on a spiritual or cultural level. When I launched my novel, *Centre of the Labyrinth*, a historical romance set in Jamaica, my daughter chose a Jamaican cultural theme for the party, got flyers, brochures and other informational material form the Jamaican Embassy located in New York. She included readings from Jamaican folklorist, Louise Bennett, and of course, my son-in-law served his deliciously made traditional Jamaican dishes. I totally sold out all the books I had ordered for the launch and got prepaid orders for others.

Similarly, when my daughter, Shauna Jamieson Carty and her husband Ricky Carty launched their book, *By Faith: A Marriage Building Devotional*, at our church they prepared for the book launch by asking their audience, in advance of the launch, to submit their wedding photographs. They then used the photographs, with appropriate music, and some narration to create a video which they used as the focal point of their book launch. It personalized the experience for everyone and the message was powerful.

Access Your Local Community

- ➢ Take your book to the local libraries and community organization, and local businesses. Host readings and book signings in your

neighborhood. Go to community events such as street fairs.
- Access community book stores. Independent book stores are usually willing to host your book signing for a percentage of the sale generated. And don't be intimidated by major chains like the Barnes and Nobles in your neighborhood.. Approach them with ideas for a book event at their store. They may not shelve your self-published book but they can be persuaded to host your book signing.
- Seek out local book clubs, local newspapers and magazines.
- Support a cause. I used my novel, "A Margin of Hope" to promote and support autism awareness locally and internationally. Its message of hope also resonated with breast cancer survivors and others.
- Team up with local authors to host a joint community book event.
- Start a local book club or meet-up group that is genre-specific (romance writers, Christian writers) or reader-specific (Teens, seniors, etc)

Take Your Book on the Road

- Most of the events / promotional activities listed under local community can be repeated beyond your local community.
- Seek out Book Expos and Conferences and Trade Shows and attend as your budget permits.
- Create your own book tour. Start with cities and states where you have family members or friends. Prepare and send your publicity tools in advance and work with your contact person (family or friend) to spread the word and secure the venue.

Your Author Website

This is a good way of maintaining your presence on the web. The primary purpose of your website should not be for selling your books. Provide tips and resources for your readers and other writers. It's your home on the Web where others can reach you. Make it user-friendly, interesting, informative, and inspiring. Feature causes that you care about and groups you support. Share information and support other authors. Bond with your readers. Show you appreciate their support not only in words, but with the occasional give-aways and free gifts.

Must-Have Promotional Tools

Your Publicity Kit. This is a powerful tool to help you build author credibility and make a great first impression with media or industry representatives. Include
- presentation folder
- Color copy of your book cover
- One-page summary of your book
- Author's bio
- Positive comments and endorsements
- Suggested interview questions
- Full color sales flyer featuring book cover. Include book synopsis and all primary and ordering information
- Set of full color post cards
- Author's Business Card

Other Promotional Tools
- Targeted mailing list for both email and regular mail
- Business Cards
- Bookmarks
- Sales flyers
- Postcards
- Tabletop displays and signs
- Bookplate

Many people have reservations about promoting their own work, assuming that others may consider them boastful. In promoting a book you have written or some other creative work you are not really promoting yourself. Your work has a purpose and a message that someone needs to get Through your creative work you are passing on to others useful information, instructions, encouragement, motivation, inspiration, etc. It's about the message – what the reader will takeaway – not about you.

My Notes

_____
_____
_____
_____
_____

Last Words

How can we understand the road we travel? It is the Lord who directs our steps.
Proverbs 20:24

Writing, publishing and marketing your book is not free. Whatever publishing path you take, it will cost you some money and a significant investment of your time. Therefore, it is important for you to establish who you are as a writer-publisher and what your writing, publishing and marketing goals are, and create a budget based on these goals.

You need a Budget and Publishing Path

In this book I have presented a do-it-yourself path to writing, publishing and marketing your books. That does not mean you have to do everything yourself. What is important here is that instead of laying out large sums of money in advance for getting your book published and coming up with more money to buy, ship, store and market your books, you can choose a publishing path that allows you to determine what you can do yourself and what you want to pay others to do for you. You have the options of taking some time to research, discover and use the many publishing tools that are available online to help you reach your publishing goals in a cost effective and profitable way. Make no mistake. This is a time-consuming and challenging approach and you may choose not to use this path. It all comes down to your vision and goals for your writing.

Some Budget Items for a DIY Path

- Your company registration fee
- ISBN & Barcode
- Copyright Registration

- Manuscript preparation fee (if you hire a freelance editor and designer/ or use the professional services offered by sites like CreateSpace for editing and cover design)
- Publishing fee ($0.00 on CreateSpace; a refundable $49.00 on IngramSpark)
- Online publishing (e-books) $0.00
- Print books (Cost of printing only. Using POD you can print one or more)
- Shipping cost
- Book promotion tools
- Book events
- Reviews (paid reviews if desired)

I hope this book has encouraged and challenged you to be the independent author-publisher you are meant to be. The information, suggestions and recommendations made throughout this book relate specifically to what my daughter and I do and experience as independent author-publishers. We encourage you to try our methods and see if they work for you. We do not expect you to take our suggestions and advice as the only way to prepare and publish your book. There is no one-size-fits-all method of publication in this business.

It is important for every self-publishing author to understand the publishing process, and the options and opportunities available, but in the long run your choice is dictated by your goals, vision and commitment. This that we offer you is a starting point in your journey - not the final word. If you are a new author or one who has been paying expensive up-front cost to publish your books and struggling to find additional money to buy your books from a "vanity press" or self-publishing service company, as well as paying marketing and promotion costs, I hope you will find this information helpful. As technology advances so do the possibilities, and the best any independent author-publisher can do is to recognize what works best for you and develop your own strategies.

Finally, you have no excuse for not taking full control of your creative work and successfully utilize the free publishing opportunities available to you. Shauna and I wish you huge success in your writing and publishing business. Strive for excellence which, "in any art or profession is only attained by hard and persistent work."(Theodore Martin), and never lose sight of the fact that, 'human excellence means nothing unless it works with the consent of God." (Euripides). And to His Glory.

RESOURCES

http://www.copyright.gov

http://creativecommons.org

http://www.nj.gov./njbusiness

http://ingramspark.com/portal/HowItworks

http://www.createspace.com

https://www.myidentifiers.com/isbn/main

http://www.socialmediaexaminer.com

http://selfpublishingnews.com

http://www.goodreads.com

Chicago Manual of Style, University of Chicago Press

Merriam Webster's Collegiate Dictionary, Springfield, MA

Crawford & Murray, *The Writer's Legal Guide,* 3rd ed., Allworth Press, NY

Mark Levine, *The Fine Print of Self-Publishing,* Kindle Edition

Ross & Ross, *Complete Guide to Self-Publishing,* Writers Digest Books

My Notes

ABOUT THE AUTHOR

Rosetta Jamieson-Thomas is an educator, author, and independent publisher. She holds a B.A. in English, Masters in Education, and M.A. in Creative Writing. She is founder and president of SBC-Christian Writers Ministry, and member of Faith Writers International. Rosetta encourages and supports aspiring writers, offers writing workshops and individualized writing courses for independent authors and others who want to hone their writing skills. She teaches Church school, serves on her church's advisory committee, and participates in community outreach ministries.

Rosetta worked for several years in the field of education holding the positions of high school teacher, teacher educator, College Lecturer, and Curriculum Specialist. She also worked for twenty-five years in a nonprofit organization where she had the challenging and very rewarding responsibility of managing a program that creates a place of hope for individuals with disabilities, and was able to make a difference in their lives – one person at a time.

Rosetta's work and her faith inspire her writing. Her novels explore the universal themes of abiding love, faith and hope as they portray characters facing life's challenges, overcoming crisis, building lasting relationships, and achieving the impossible through faith in God. Her devotional writings are testimonies to the faithful of God in the lives of His people.

Contact Rosetta at christianwriters200@yahoo.com

Website: https://www.empoweredpages.com

Other Books from Rosetta Jamieson-Thomas

Devotional & Inspirational Books

GREEN PASTURES :
A Collection of Devotionals, Testimonies and Reflections

Does God really care about our routine daily activities? In today's world are peace and security really possible? Inspired by Psalm 23, this collection of personal experiences and triumphs is one congregation's testimony to the fact that God does make provisions for the moment-by-moment situations in the life of His people, and no matter what we are facing, He is always there for us.

"Green Pastures is an inspiring work. By listening to the collective heartbeat of one local congregation, this book provides all of us with a practical, thoughtful perspective for daily living. The contributing writers courageously confront the ups and downs of the human experience. This is an awesome offering that celebrates our awesome God!"
- Dr. Glen E. Porter

STILL WATERS:
A Treasury of Faith Stories for Daily Meditation

This is the second publication in the devotional book series inspired by Psalm 23. It is the collective work of a congregation that has experienced, through faith, the blessings of walking with God in the light of His word. In this devotional book Christians of all ages share their journey to finding peace with God, and can joyously say with the Psalmist David, *"The Lord is my Shepherd. . . . he leadeth me beside still waters. He restoreth my soul."*

Do you need a pick-me-up? A spiritual boost to uplift and refresh your spirit? Get a copy of these powerful devotional books for moments when you need to encourage yourself.

Rosetta's Novels

A Margin of Hope

A Margin of Hope is a contemporary Christian Romance novel set in the USA. In this novel, Rosetta Jamieson-Thomas weaves together themes of love, faith, and hope with the harsh realities of the immigrant's struggle to achieve the American dream.

A Margin of Hope is the story of Vanessa Jones, a single mother who puts her personal dreams on hold to raise her son, Andrew, who is diagnosed with autism. Follow Vanessa on each leg of her faith-journey from Jamaica to Florida and New York. See her struggles. Feel her pain. Laugh with her. Experience with her the emotional impact of her reunion with Moses Richardson, Andrew's father, after seven years of separation, and the tension as she is torn between her passion for Moses and her commitment to another man. Can love, faith and hope sustain her in the decisions she must make as she faces Moses rejection of their autistic son, the wrath of the other woman in Moses' life, and the act of revenge that threatens to destroy her world?

"For the reader who appreciates a touching novel covering every aspect of humanity – love, hate, romance, religion, jealousy, emotional wisdom - then A Margin of Hope is waiting. ---This book, undoubtedly will find its way on the shelf of this reviewer's special novels that find their way into a reader's heart." Bea Smith, Arts & Leisure, Union County Local Source, New Jersey

Centre of the Labyrinth

Centre of the Labyrinth is a historical romance novel set on the beautiful island of Jamaica in the early 1960's. Young and romantic, the hero and heroine, Robert Laeton and Deita Folkes, strived for perfect love only to find that ultimately they must face a crisis of identity that threatens to destroy all they found together and held dear. Robert, the son of the Busha Massa and heir to the Laeton's fortune, is being groomed to take over leadership of the village. Deita is the daughter of a mentally unstable woman and maid to the Laetons. Their love is socially forbidden, and their relationship is challenged by Lloyd Benjamin, Robert's cousin who wants both the Laeton's legacy and Deita's love.

"Centre of the Labyrinth is an emotional story with strong impact, which will certainly stay with the readers long after they finish the book."-- Writer's Digest

"Wow! That was fantastic. I thoroughly enjoyed Centre of the Labyrinth. I hope it will be made into a movie." Mark. Ontario, Canada

A five-star read!" – Sophia, Houston, TX, USA

Books by Shauna Jamieson Carty

The Heart to Love
By Shauna Jamieson Carty

   When a teenage boy says he has the heart to love a girl for the rest of their lives, can she believe him? Wendy's mother believed Wendy's father and ended up pregnant and alone. Now Wendy is 17 years old and saving herself for her high school sweetheart Paul. Paul promises to marry her after graduation and enter a covenant of everlasting love. Wendy's mother withholds her blessings and cautions them to wait. Now Wendy is about to find out where her father stands: beside her as she walks down the aisle or by her mother.

The Heart to Live
By Shauna Jamieson Carty

 College life isn't the "happily ever after" that Wendy and Paul dreamed of when they were in high school. They attend the same university, but nothing seems to be going according to their plans. "Remember to pray for me," Paul tells Wendy. Wendy covers Paul with her prayers, but their security is shattered and depression sets in because of a tragic shooting on their college campus. Will sharing their faith help to restore the peace and give them and their peers the heart to live joyfully again?

The Heart to Forgive
By Shauna Jamieson Carty

Love is everlasting, except of course when our loved ones hurt our feelings and it's just too hard to forgive. At the center of Paul and Wendy's faith is the belief that they can pray to God and ask for forgiveness for the things they have done wrong. God will forgive them and they must forgive others. They and their friends Constance and Sergio pursue different paths after college, but they share a common loss and continue to get together for a memorial benefit concert once a year. Can they get past the pain of hurtful relationships? Will they have the heart to forgive themselves and each other and embrace God's unfailing love?

Praying in the Moment

Praying in the Moment: Reflections on the Election of President Barack Obama, by Shauna Jamieson Carty, spans the generations. Eight of the reflections are told through the eyes of Americans who have experienced race relations at its worst, but have now lived to witness progress beyond many of their expectations. The ninth reflection documents the experience of a young adult who attended the inauguration. The tenth gives voice to three children under age ten who express how they feel about the election of America's first black president.

By Faith

By Faith: A Marriage Building Devotional with prayers, activities, and discussion topics, by Ricky and Shauna Carty, conveys the perspective that a lasting, happy and faithful marriage is a gift from God for which we should glorify Him, and not a direct construction of man for which we should credit ourselves. It can be used as an individual or couples' devotional, or it can be a workbook for married couples whereby they can record their own stories and store keepsakes as a legacy of the Christian marriage for younger generations.

Rosetta and Shauna's books are available on Amazon.com and/ or directly from the authors.

Author Website: https://www.empoweredpages.com

Email: Christianwriters200@yahoo.com

Email: island_novel@yahoo.com

All proceeds from sale of the Devotional Books and from *Praying in the Moment* go to Second Baptist Church, Roselle, NJ 07203.

My Notes

From Idea to Publication

www.ingramcontent.com/pod-product-compliance
Lightning Source LLC
LaVergne TN
LVHW021410080426
835508LV00020B/2533